Songs from My Soul

POEMS & ESSAYS OF HEALING

Grace Miglio Pearce

HAMPSHIRE PRESS
GLEN HEAD, NEW YORK

Grateful acknowledgement is made for permission to reprint lyrics from the song "Get Together." Words and music by Chet Powers. Copyright © 1963 by IRVING MUSIC INC. Copyright renewed. All rights reserved. Reprinted by permission of Hal Leonard LLC.

Copyright © 2025 by Grace Miglio Pearce. All rights reserved. No part of this publication may be reproduced, distributed, or transmitted in any form or by any means, including photocopying, recording, or other electronic or mechanical methods, without the prior written permission of the publisher, except in the case of brief quotations embodied in critical reviews and certain other noncommercial uses permitted by copyright law. For permission requests, contact the author at the website below.

Hampshire Press / Grace Miglio Pearce
Website: gracemigliopearce.com

Cover painting © by Erin Spencer
Cover design by Gus Yoo
Editing and production by Stephanie Gunning

Songs from My Soul / Grace Miglio Pearce
—1st edition

ISBN 979-8-9927379-0-5 (paperback)
ISBN 979-8-9927379-1-2 (kindle ebook)

To my soul mate, Matt.

To everyone who is examining and searching: May you connect with the deepest part of your soul, and be filled with much peace, joy, and love.

CONTENTS

Preface ix

Winter Woods *3*

Pink Primulas *5*

Matthew *6*

What's the Rush? *8*

The Grief That Lives Inside *10*

Awakening *12*

The Sea and Me *14*

Slow Me Down *16*

All the Light That I Can See *18*

A Forest of Light *19*

Long Dresses: Essay *20*

My Sisters and Me *27*

Cows and the A272 *29*

SONGS FROM MY SOUL

When Time Stands Still *31*

Six Observations in My Garden Today *33*

My Friend Kim *35*

Instructions *38*

Aunt Lulu *40*

Winter Blues *43*

Clementine *44*

Sleeping Beauty #1 *46*

Salvatore: Essay *47*

Loving You *49*

The Friends Who Lit My Way *51*

Bare Branches *53*

Sometimes *54*

Sleeping Beauty #2 *55*

Your Eyes *57*

Belonging *59*

GRACE MIGLIO PEARCE

Stillness *61*

Celestial Blue *63*

Amazing Grace and Juliet *65*

The Miracle of Trees *68*

Healing *71*

Notes 75

Acknowledgments 76

About the Author 85

PREFACE

"The unexamined life is not worth living."
SOCRATES

For most of us, there comes a point where we start to examine the meaning of our existence more closely. Such examination usually occurs after a major life event like a trauma, the death of a loved one, an illness, or becoming an empty-nester. The initiating event causes us so much pain, such deep pain, that we feel as if we have only two choices: the choice either to shut ourselves off from our feelings entirely or to let the pain break us open and remodel the structure of our being. Allowing the pain to touch us, we look inside and begin to question everything we've been taught and believed—perhaps since we were children.

For me, a deep search for meaning started when my father passed away. My whole heart cracked wide open from grief and I started to question everything I thought I knew, especially the existence of God. The nature and presence of God. Soon, I could no longer attend a Catholic mass without feeling an uncontrollable urge to scream.

The last time I attended mass is when it happened. The liturgy felt robotic and empty: Stand up, sit down, kneel, recite the Lord's Prayer, the Apostles' Creed . . . I looked around me in complete shock at the banality of the ritual I had performed so many times before, and wanted to shout, "Please, can we speak with some love and emotion? Can we sing with passion and grace?"

I wanted to ask, "Is anyone else feeling what I'm feeling?" But I did none of those things. It seemed more depressing than a funeral.

By the end of the mass, I was bursting at my emotional seams and could no longer contain my frustration. And then it happened. As all of the other "mourners" were exiting their pews, I felt a rebellious energy bubbling up inside me, rising from my stomach all the way to my mouth. Not being able to control my frustration a minute longer, I took a deep breath and felt my mouth open. I was expecting something loud and ugly to come out, but the sound that came forth was soft and meek at the start.

I was sweating and could feel knots in my stomach. But I shut my eyes and breathed in and out, and out came the most beautiful *Ave* and then an impassioned *Maria*. And I was off—there would be no turning back. With my eyes closed and standing completely still in my pew, I sang; and as I sang, I could feel all the layers of my heart opening until I was filled with immense joy and gratitude.

Ave Maria, Ave Maria
Ave, Ave
Ave Maria, Ave Maria
Ave, Ave
Ave Maria, Ave Maria
Ave, Ave
Ave Maria, Ave Maria
Ave, Ave

Somewhere in the middle of singing, I opened my eyes and noticed the men of the congregation looking at me strangely, not knowing what to do with someone who had the temerity to treat the church service as if it were a Broadway show.

They simply walked away from me.

The women, however, stayed. They stayed, and at the end of the song, they thanked me and surrounded me with love. One beautiful soul reached out for my hands and as she held them tightly, she looked deep into my eyes and said, "I needed this today. Thank you so much. You have filled me with so much joy." I could feel tears beginning to stream down my cheeks. My heart was full and I hugged her.

All I could think in that moment was, *'Why don't we have more of this in the Church? This connection with one another. This opening of our hearts and our souls—this is what's missing.'*

My search for deeper meaning has often steered me to the feminine side of the Christian narrative. Soon after my church experience, I was drawn to read *Mary Magdalene Revealed* by Meggan Waterson, and to research the Gnostic Gospel of Mary Magdalene. Although there are many pages missing from her gospel, its message is clear: The divine lives in each of us and we can connect to our soul, our divinity, by turning within. I realized that this was what was missing for me in the Church. It was the complete opposite of what I had been taught. I was conditioned to adhere to a higher authority and to look outside myself.

And this is what the Gospel of Mary Magdalene is all about: the Christ within us. As I sang in church, I connected to the divine within myself and Mother Mary. My heart opened, and I felt a beautiful connection with all the women who stayed with me and they with each other.

I do believe that Christ wanted us to go within, and that the true message of Christ is that we are made of the divine. Although our institutions may have somehow missed it, culturally we are slowly finding our way back to recognition of the Christ that lives inside each of us. He wanted us to go within to form that deep connection with ourselves, and to one another.

SONGS FROM MY SOUL

This understanding is where my poems come from. They are written from the deepest place in my soul. It feels as if they are being channeled from within me. Being in nature plays a big part in my ability to connect within. I began taking walks in the woods, doing tree meditations, sitting meditations, and slowed my breath and my mind down. I would often talk to the trees and the flowers and greet them with a sense of joy and wonder. On my departure, I would be mindful to thank them for their presence and for helping me ground myself.

It was about this time that I happened upon a video of the poet Coleman Barks interviewing the poet Mary Oliver. I had never read any of her poems or heard of her before then, but what she said struck me as powerfully true.

> *So many of us live most of our lives seeking the answerable and somehow demeaning or bypassing those things that can't be answered and therefore denuding one's life of the acceptance of mystery and the pleasure of mystery and the willingness to live with mystery is greatly what I think about*

GRACE MIGLIO PEARCE

and if I could do something for people I would say don't forget the mystery, love the mystery, be glad of it, don't want answers all the time.[1]

I can't even begin to describe how her words took a lifetime of pressure off me. They gave me permission not to have all the answers, to embrace the mystery of life, and to let life unfold naturally.

Spending time in nature has slowed me down—slowed my breath, my thoughts, my whole being—and it has allowed me to live in the moment. When we live in the moment, we are able to see and hear what is right in front of us, and that's when magic happens. We don't have to figure it all out. We can just let life unfold without any expectations or pressure. By embracing the mystery of life, we open ourselves up to wonder, adventure, and imagination. When I let go of the need to have all of the answers my poems came flowing out of me.

I approach my faith differently now. The nuns from my childhood put the fear of God in me instead of helping me build a deep connection to Christ. I was made to feel inferior to all of the male figures controlling the Church and taught to look for the sacred outside of myself. Deep down I have always known this was wrong, and I don't want to lose myself anymore. We can only find ourselves if we go within.

I have done my best to mitigate the influence on my psyche of concepts like *sin*, which the Church is into, along with a bunch of prescriptive *supposed tos, thou shalts,* and *thou shalt nots.* Letting go of rigid expectations has been glorious and wonderful. I am free. Hurrah! Although the grace I experience on occasion does not last long, it has made me determined to find out if it would be possible to live my life in peace and grace long term. My walks in nature and the meditation I do in the woods and by the ocean are helping me heal.

It's not an overnight fix to undo all of the conditioning I've had since childhood. But the beautiful thing is that I now believe it is most certainly possible. The more awake and connected we are to ourselves and each other the better we feel. We are living in a magnificent time of deep awakening and change, and we have the ability to heal and to touch each other's lives with our love and kindness. Even our messy moments teach us valuable lessons. I am trying to communicate lessons that I learn and observations about life and nature through my poetry.

Perhaps the ultimate healing for me is how, finally, after so many years of not believing in my creative gifts or myself, I have found the confidence to listen to the call of my creative self, of my soul, and to answer it fully, without limitation or fear. It took me decades, but I got there in the end.

When I used to think, *I am getting older and I haven't lived my dreams yet. What if I never follow my dreams?* I'd feel regret. But now I wake up in the morning and smile because I am living my dreams.

Writing my poems is a dream that I lovingly share with you.

Songs from My Soul

WINTER WOODS

I took a walk in the winter woods and was
    surprised by what I found there.
With no expectations, no preconceived notions
    of what I would find,
I just followed a voice that beckoned me:
    'Come, walk.'

As I made my way along the wood-chipped path,
I smiled to hear my feet make a loud crunching
    sound.
It satisfied me in the most peculiar way.
Crunch, crunch, crunch—I couldn't get enough
    of this gratifying sound.

I jumped, skipped, stomped, and hopped
    down the winding path.
'Take this, take that,' my feet seemed to say.
This solid sensation was a welcome release
    from all that was troubling me.

As I arrived at the edge of the woods, I turned
    back for a parting glance.

Standing completely still, I looked up in awe at
the trees and said to them,
'You are so high you seem to reach the clear
blue sky.'
'Oh, but we do, we do,' they responded
in unison
with a powerful gust of wind that danced
through their bare branches,
as if waving goodbye. 'We hope to see you
again very soon!'

Just ahead of me, a ray of light broke through
the trees, and shone down
upon a clearing filled with an endless blanket
of pure white snowdrops.
Like rows and rows of tiny angels welcoming me,
they went on and on and on with no end
in sight.

PINK PRIMULAS

'You must go, write your poems:
Be bold, BE BOLD,' I heard her say,
in her Mary Oliver way.
Nothing is certain,
so what do you care?
The perfect pink primulas,
in all their loveliness,
are on the verge of blooming.
This is what matters.
Not anything else.
Be careful not to miss it.

MATTHEW

Thank you for coming to find me again.
Although I didn't realize it at the time,
    I had lost you.
When I first saw you standing by the jukebox
    fumbling with your change,
You caught my eye.
There was something about you.
I was impressed by your crisp, carefully ironed
    blue and white checkered shirt.
(Don't ask me why I was impressed,
    I haven't a clue. All I knew was that there
    was something about you that pulled me to
    you like a magnet, so I approached you.)
It wasn't until years later that my soul recognized
    our connection.
It hit me all of a sudden, like a thunderbolt,
    After years of working on myself,
    Connecting within,
    And finally overcoming my conditioning,
I know him!
I suddenly found you deep within my heart,
where you have always been,

And always will be.
Of this, I'm sure: We have had many lives
 together,
And from this life to the next, and in the one
 after that,
We will discover each other all over again.
*I will always breathe life into you, and you
 into me,*
So please, always come find me.

WHAT'S THE RUSH?

I sit silently in a chair by my window and
    stare at the snow.
I wonder aloud, 'Where did my father go?
This vibrant man,
I see him everywhere and I can't let go.
I hear him calling out my name,
    'Grace Ann, Grace Ann.'
I feel him when I watch a film and someone dies
and all I can do is cry and cry, and then I
    wonder,
'Where DID my father go?
And why did he leave us all so soon?'
Before the sun fully rose
on that hot, balmy day,
in the stillness of the quietest hour
he passed away.
And all this time I thought he'd last,
    just a while longer.
'Can't you linger, Daddy?
What's the rush?' I would've asked.

'The sea is calm,
the birds not yet singing.
The air is fresh and oh so still,
and you love it here.
You love the bay and the way the gentle waves
    invite us all to breathe.
You love the rugged stone that lines the shore.
You love the soothing sand that caresses our feet
when we stand knee deep in the restorative
    salt water.
You love the joyful swims we've had
filled with endless splashing and laughter.
You love the conversations, chest deep in water,
in which time stands still, with cousins, nephews,
    brothers, daughters big and small.
But most of all,
you love and feel the soul within this place.
For this is home.'

THE GRIEF THAT LIVES INSIDE

Do not lie to me for a minute longer.
Grief does not pass and get better with time.

'It comes and goes in waves,' you say.
Well, that may be true for some, but not
    for me.
My grief is like an unconstrained dam
whose pent-up water gushes through its
    opening
with so much rage and so much fury.

But once a dam's water is released, it is free.
True for the water, but not for me.

I am wild and riotous.
I rage against the sky.
My grief cannot be contained,
nor can it be set free.
It lives inside every part of me,
for that's how much he meant to me.

So, no, no, do not try to make me see
    a different way to feel my pain.
No words could ever explain the grief that lives
    inside me.

AWAKENING

It's okay if you are better than me,
it really is fine.
I'm letting go, I don't have the time.
I'm not good at this,
this real estate.
Proving our cleverness, how smart can we be?
Who can negotiate a shrewder deal, you or me?
I've had enough,
I'm stepping away.
I'm no longer here to play
these games, because they drain every ounce of
    what's good in me.
They take away my light, and my sanity
and all that is good with humanity.
I'm better than this time-wasting paradigm
that cleverly steals (like a thief in the night)
all that is mine.
This pattern is shifting, it's going away.
You win, I'm out. Hurrah, hooray.
I will no longer stay.
I will no longer stay in this soul-crushing place.

You are better than me and that really is fine
because I simply. don't. have. the. time.

THE SEA AND ME

I am fascinated by the sea,
And I wonder if the sea is awed by me.
Are you, Sea?
Do you think as highly of me as I do of you?
Do you feel my sorrow emanating from my
    toes while I'm sinking them into your
    soothing, wet sand?
Do you understand how good this feels?

Can you see the tears streaming down my face
    as I release in your presence, feeling safe in
    the body of you?
Do you feel my breathing normalize as I tune in
    to the rhythmic pulse of your waves,
    moving in and out, in and out,
    as if in a meditative trance?
Can you feel all of my stress melting away—
Or are you too busy, flowing, foaming, creating,
Various hues of brilliant blue,

Whose tint depends on the way the sun shines
   on you?

SLOW ME DOWN

I may be one but I am strong
and I know now where I belong.
Give me the trees, the sun, the bay,
    mountains, hills,
I shall not stray.
Place me amongst God's beauteous flowers
and I shall sit for hours.

Slow me down, slow me down.
That's where all the answers lie:
In life's quiet breath.
In and out, in and out.
I quiet my mind so I may breathe
    gentle, easy breaths.
In and out.
Slow, slow, slow.

Let me breathe. Oh, let me breathe,
    so I may explore my soul.
'You are free, you are free,' is her message to me.

I know where I belong.
I may be one, but I am strong.
And I now know where I belong.
I am free.

ALL THE LIGHT THAT I CAN SEE

All the light that I can see
lives deep inside of me.
So, if you need a kind word spoken,
some comfort given,
a heartfelt hug,
you can rely on me,
for I shall pay no attention to the polarity
that permeates our world today.

When the world is upside down,
when there are no smiles to be found,
no laughter, no joy,
when hate-filled anger has taken over the internet,
and there is immense danger looming
    of me getting down,
I shall remember the light that I can see
which lives, always, in the deepest part of me,
and I will keep to my stride.

A FOREST OF LIGHT

Let me stay awhile in this forest of light and
    soak up all its peaceful goodness.
Let me listen to the whispers of my soul
    as I linger in this sacred sanctuary.
I can hear the gentle rustle of the trees dancing
    with the wind,
And singing songs of love and joy.
In nature, I receive the answers I don't have
    to so many questions.
Now, as I breathe deep, soulful breaths,
    the most important answer comes to me.
I hear a life-changing whisper, 'It's okay not
    to know,
Okay not to have the answers to all of life's
    great mysteries.'
I don't know why I thought I had to figure it
    out in the first place!
There is an unexpected, wonderful freedom in
    accepting what is.
As my realization sinks in,
I marvel at the beautiful place where
    I have found myself.

LONG DRESSES

Come on people now
Smile on your brother
Everybody get together
Try to love one another
Right now.

These were the words I chose for my high school yearbook. They were lyrics from the mid-60's song 'Get Together,' made famous by the Youngbloods. I remember feeling nervous about my choice, worried what my classmates would think. At seventeen, I was scared and filled with so many different emotions. School had not been an easy road for me, as I never felt safe or accepted. I had been subjected to an 'I hate Grace club,' in fourth grade when I first transferred to Holy Child from my old school. Well, none of my classmates was holy. Not by a long shot. For years after my arrival, I was overweight and constantly belittled and teased by my peers.

In fifth grade, I was overjoyed when a classmate of mine called me on the phone (this had never happened before then) to let me know that all the girls would be wearing long dresses that coming Friday and to make sure I wore my maxi dress. I remember feeling excited when I got off the phone and my happiness was contagious. My mother, smiling from ear to ear, eagerly ironed my long dress and ribbons.

The next morning couldn't come soon enough. I awoke at 6 AM excited for the day to start. My mother lovingly brushed and styled my hair, pulling it gently away from my face, and placed a gorgeous white silk ribbon on the back of my head. I went to school with a bounce in my step, and felt like a beautiful princess.

I couldn't contain my excitement when I arrived at school, I was singing and full of hope. I felt beautiful in my multicolored checkered dress that featured a lovely white lace trim on both the hem and waist. I admired every last detail. But when I opened the door to my classroom my heart immediately sank. The other girls (every single one of them) were wearing short dresses, the complete opposite of what I had been told. My shoulders dropped and I lowered my head trying as hard as I could to be invisible while walking as fast as humanly possible to my desk. My classmates were all whispering and giggling, with their hands covering their mouths.

The hardest part of my day was facing my mother when I got home. She had been so happy for me that I didn't want to disappoint her. I felt so ashamed, as if it were something I had done.

Elementary school never got any better for me. I wish I could say that I experienced a major transformation and woke up one morning not caring what anyone thought of me, but this wasn't the case. High school was a little better, I had met a lovely girl while riding our bikes Out East one summer and we became fast friends. Although she hadn't attended the same elementary school as me, she was by my side for three out of my four years in high school. I honestly don't know what I would have done without her friendship. The nuns weren't the friendliest. And the popular girls were extremely cliquey and not at all inclusive. Us less popular girls lived in fear of those girls.

In hindsight, I don't know why I had felt so intimidated, it was as if my self-esteem was dependent on them liking me. I recently saw a photo of a group of them on Facebook, out to lunch, all smiling and happy. I thought about friending those middle-aged women and imagined what it would be like to join them at one of their luncheons. Instantly, a knot formed in my stomach and my whole body tensed up. All my ancient feelings of insecurity and not being accepted returned and I was transported back to high school. *'Hmmm, maybe it wouldn't be such a good idea for me to reach out to them,'* I acknowledged.

'The reality is that I would likely never be accepted by them, not even now. This is okay with me. I am relieved to be able to stop considering the possibility because I don't think I would enjoy their company. And I probably wouldn't have enjoyed being friends back in high school much either—if they had accepted me.' I let that sink in.

I got accused once of cheating on a religion exam. A childhood 'friend' asked me for a pencil, but I couldn't hear what she was saying at first so I asked her what she needed. Next thing I knew, I was seated in the principal's office being accused of cheating by Sister Ann. My friend not only got my pencil, but she was allowed to finish her exam. She didn't get punished.

When I went back a couple of years later to let this steely nun know that, in fact, I had not cheated, to my disappointment, she looked at me blankly and said, 'I don't remember.'

Well, I remembered.

I lost a lot of weight in tenth grade and started getting noticed by the boys. The problem was, one of the popular girls' boyfriend kept throwing snowballs at me to get my attention. Because the last thing I wanted was to be hated more than I already was by the cool group, I ignored his advances and kept to myself. But deep down I was so darn pleased to be liked by such a good-looking boy—even if it meant receiving dirty looks from all of the popular girls.

I did start dating a handsome boy when I was fifteen, but when he didn't turn up for my sweet sixteen party (I spent most of my party looking for him out the window) I broke up with him. Turned out he was seeing someone else behind my back, so that was a good call by me.

It wasn't until after I graduated, and went on to attend university that things came together for me. I met an amazing group of friends some of whom I'm still close with today.

Reflecting back on why I chose the lyrics I chose for my yearbook quote: It is because I wanted to express my personal commitment to be loving and kind. It's not easy to love people who aren't kind, and who, in fact, go out of their way to be mean—no matter what their age.

But we can try. And I think that's why the lyrics of the song are 'TRY to love one another right now,' as opposed to 'love one another right now.'

None of us is perfect. I know I personally have a strong response to injustice and will go into flight-or-fight mode in uncomfortable situations, especially when I'm being confronted.

My husband has asked me on occasion, 'Are you looking for a fight?'

'No,' I respond, 'I just want everyone to wear their long dresses.'

MY SISTERS AND ME

I dreamed I was one of the Three Graces in
    Botticelli's *Primavera*.
(I like to visit this painting, now and then, to
    convince myself that I don't have to adjust
    to society's norms of skinny and trim.)
We're doing a slow, meditative dance, touching
    hands, floating as if in a trance.
Twirling in see-through dresses that
    unabashedly show the curves and beauty of
    our voluptuous bodies, we haven't a single
    care for what anyone thinks.

Go away, all you skinny models in magazines,
    you have tormented me long enough—
    we are free, we are free, my sisters and me.
Floating, dancing, without a care, with our
    long, wavy, sun-kissed hair.
Comfortable. Happy with our curvy hips and
    insatiable thighs, our well-rounded breasts,
    and all the rest.
We are free, we *are* free, my sisters and me.

In our full-bodied selves, we are most certainly free.

COWS AND THE A272

As we were driving along the A272 toward
    Winchester this morning,
I spotted a large group of black cows with
    varying patterns of white spots.
They were lying all huddled together on the
    lush, green grass.
And I wondered, *'Are cows social animals?*
    Do they plan to meet up like this? Or is this
    a spontaneous occurrence?'
Perhaps this was their version of a ladies' coffee
    morning.
I smiled to myself as I imagined all sorts of
    fanciful conversations they would be having
    with each other.
There was an enviable peacefulness about the
    way they lay there, so calm and content,
    without a worry in the world.
No fighting, no judgment, just being with
    each other in agreeable silence.

As the sun shone down on them in its most calming way, I thought to myself,
'I should pay more attention to what these cows are saying.'

WHEN TIME STANDS STILL

How do I say goodbye to you,
You who've known me since before I was born?
Your light, your love, has shone upon me
    my whole, entire life.
And though it's nearing the time when you
    shall bid farewell,
You are not weary, yet.

Linger upon this good earth a while longer,
For you have people to see and there are
    espressos that need brewing—
Prepared so lovingly whenever one calls around.
'Straight up or with a shot of sambuca?' I hear
    you ask,
Secretly hoping this will not be our last.

Is it my imagination or is everything particularly
    beautiful today?
Has time stood still?

Does the grass not look greener?
Does the birdsong not sound more joyous than
 ever before?
Are the roses and hydrangeas not more vibrant
 and colorful?
I take it all in, everything!

The world seems especially magical
 in this moment,
And I think it's because you and the Universe
 are in cahoots:
You've arranged an extra special day for us.
Let's not ruin it by saying goodbye.

SIX OBSERVATIONS IN MY GARDEN TODAY

Today I noticed, for the very first time . . .

1.

The vibrant red leaves on the photinia sprouting upward with a lot of confidence. 'I'm so happy to be here!' they seemed to say, as they gently swayed back and forth in the light, airy breeze.

2.

An indistinguishable bird gliding peacefully above me carrying a large, strangely shaped twig in her beak, determined to lay it upon her ever-growing nest.

3.

A trio of blackbirds swirling in the sky making quite a racket and finally settling on three separate branches.

4.

Two pigeons continuously annoying one another. *'Is one trying to mate the other?'* I wondered to myself.

5.

A sweet little robin building her nest in a rather dull-colored birdhouse that was once a vibrant yellow and blue.

6.

A big, plump, buzzing bumblebee dancing and whizzing here and there without a care.

I was curious to know if all these living creatures noticed that this was the first sunny day we've had in quite a while. I'm sure they must have, because never have I seen such busyness in my garden.

At least not for a very long time.

MY FRIEND KIM

I received a call today letting me know that a
    friend from long ago had passed away.
This is happening more and more these days.
I remember my friend Kim with so much
    fondness,
and recall, with sadness, the fun we had.
She gifted me two striped glasses.
It was on the eve of her move to San Diego.
They were frosted with creamsicle-colored
    stripes in shades of pastel green and pink.
I kept them for as long as I could, until
    one after the other they were broken—
The first by a family member who loaded the
    dishwasher with glasses all jammed together.
The second by me.
The glass slipped through my wet fingers and
    crashed to the ground.
I looked down in disbelief at all the beautiful,
    shattered pieces of glass and cried for hours.

I don't know why those glasses meant so much
to me.
Perhaps I cherished them because no one had
ever given me a gift with such pure love.
I felt guilty that she had spent so much money on
me, like I didn't deserve such a beautiful gift.
But she felt differently.
I remember Kim as if it were today that she was
waitressing and mopping floors with me.
We shared a stolen kiss on an old porch
she'd rented.
This was all she could afford in the height of
the summer season in the Hamptons.
I was surprised when she leaned in and did it,
but I didn't pull away.
It lasted just a moment and was gentle and sweet.
Almost apologizing, I told her, "I like boys."
She replied, "I know, me too."
Then we both looked at each other and
laughed and laughed.
We were so young.
We swam in the ocean and sat by the sea,

Rode our bikes down Main Street while Kim
    unabashedly sang 'Stairway to Heaven'
    at the top of her lungs.
If only I could be as carefree as her.
We were so young.
If only I had kept in touch.
There was so much to explore, so much more.

INSTRUCTIONS

Do not bury me in the cold, hard ground,
nor place me in a coffin where I can't make
    a sound.
No, burn me in a wicker basket covered with
    fragrant, blush-pink roses,
and place my ashes next to an ancient yew tree,
where I can speak to my new friend and
    reminisce about days gone by.

And when the weather changes and a new
    season arrives,
I shall stay right by my friend's side.
We'll enjoy the snowdrops and bluebells together,
and marvel at the miracle of spring's rebirth.

When summertime comes, as it often does,
    with so much fanfare,
Surround me with a multitude of fragrant
    flowers.
I'll wait for you under the warm and
    comforting sun.

And when a gentle breeze arises, I shall fly high
	in the sky,
dancing and swirling with all the birds,
possibly singing a song or two—or even three—
so that you will know I am free.

When you come outside to visit me
	by our wise old yew,
you can trust that my love for you
	will never die.
Whether I'm flying in the sky or sitting
	right by your side,
if you are feeling blue, you can rely on me
	to comfort you.

Yes, you can rely on me to comfort you.
For our love is forever true, and I will always,
	always be in love with you.

AUNT LULU

Is that it?
Is that all we do?
A mass, a lunch, a burial, too.
And then what?
It's not at all enough.

This was an extraordinary life, a soul,
    a beauteous being who weaved her joy
    and love into our hearts,
Whose positivity and love of dance and singing
    were contagious,
Whose light shone exceedingly bright.

A few days of mourning and then
    we are through?
No, it is not nearly enough.
I shall shout it from the mountaintops.
I shall let my feelings soar high above the sky.
    'We love you, Aunt Lulu!'

Let the trumpets sound their horns.
Call all the heavenly and earthly angels
    to gather around and celebrate
    this magnificent being—
For she's an angel, too.
But you knew that, didn't you?

With our feet firmly planted on the ground,
    our gaze to the sky,
We can see her.
We can feel her everywhere, for she is near.

It's as if she is the sea, and the sea is me.
She penetrates every part of me and
    reminds me to respond with love.
Not to lose my patience.

She is the calm on the bay.
She is a fragrant pink rose in full bloom in May.
She is the light that caresses my face on a sunny day.
She is still my Aunt Lulu.

Lulu, when I am alone,
I shall look for you in the sea
and sing a joyful song with thee.

Then we may splash together and laugh.

I remember how, one time, just when I was
> about to burst out crying, you turned to me
> with brown paper candy wrappers covering
> your teeth and I howled with laughter.

Wish you could do that for me now, because
> you've always managed to turn my sorrow
> into joy.

Because that was what you did, a few days of
> mourning for you will never suffice.

No, no, I shall take you wherever I go forever
> and ever,

And celebrate the essence of you.

WINTER BLUES

We both sat forlornly on the bed,
Both of us feeling the dread in unison.
'I don't want to swim, I don't want to talk,
    I don't even want to take a walk.'
That's what I would've said if I had spoken.

Was it the bitter-cold January air?
Or perhaps the dull gray sky was making us
    want to cry?
We sat in emotion-laden silence and pondered
    why we felt so blue.
Our mutual feelings of gloom were a perfect
    match for the weather outside.

Hope is a mere sliver of light on a cold, dark day—
Especially when the sky is full of gray.

CLEMENTINE

I wish I were like Clementine.
She is beauteous and fine—
some might even dare say *divine*.

I wish I were like Clementine,
so plump and fair,
calmly sitting, without a care,
majestic in her throne-like chair.

I wish I were like Clementine
for I'm convinced she *is* divine.
She lives the way I want to live,
unperturbed, with love to give.

The world we live in's so full of hate,
if you don't agree with what they say,
watch out for the rest of the day.

The world we live in's so full of hate,
Your heart will sink, you'll lose your way.

Words are bullets when used in anger.
There are too many flying around.

I wish I were like Clementine.
For she is beauteous and fair,
not a mean word to say about anyone.

I wish I were like Clementine.
she is like an angel that guides our way,
and fills us with hope for a brighter day.

Stay, Clementine, stay.
The world needs your grace.
And I know I speak not out of place.

SLEEPING BEAUTY #1

I might be old, but I am bold.
So excuse me if I insult your sensibilities with
    all that is inside of me.
But this sleeping beauty needs to rhyme,
And this is *my* time.

I've struggled my whole life to make a stand.
To finally, at last, do as I planned.
To yell and shout without any doubt.
To find the courage to break out.

SALVATORE

'Don't take the name *Salvatore* out of *Salvatore Ferragamo!* Why would you do this?' I asked the 30 percent-off sale ad on my iPhone.

I couldn't believe it. I checked my phone as soon as I arrived home from visiting my cousin. Despite having eliminated the name Salvatore, they had the audacity to try to tempt me with a sale. I'd been eyeing their blush-pink continental flat wallet for months, waiting for the price to be reduced. Now what was I to do?

I was deeply saddened when my cousin told me the news that they took out the name Salvatore. 'All for branding purposes,' she explained. 'It's just Ferragamo now.' I felt as if I had been punched in the gut. *Thank God my father isn't alive to witness this!* I thought.

Memories of my dad defending his name came rushing back to me. 'What's wrong with the name Salvatore?' I heard him ask. 'It's a famous name: Salvatore Ferragamo, Salvatore Ferragamo!' Over and over again, he would repeat,

'It's a beautiful name. Salvatore, Salvatore, Salvatore,' practically singing it. He wore his name, Salvatore Miglio, like a meticulously polished badge of honor on a beat-up old suit jacket that had been through countless wars and tribulations.

Deep down my father was sad that no one in our family had named their sons after him. My parents had named their first-born son after his father and their second-born son after my mother's father. For his generation, it was an act of love and respect.

I had a daughter, so I wasn't able to honor my father in that way, and I wouldn't have traded her for anything in the world, although the feeling of letting him down crushed me.

But Ferragamo was another story. That company sure has a nerve! I vowed that day never to buy anything from this designer ever again!

I don't care how enticing their next sale may be.

LOVING YOU

The Saturday morning after the Friday of
    loving you was unbearable.
While in traffic on the A3, you say,
    'We don't have much time left, so it's
    important that we're happy.'
This reality hits me hard,
the reality of how short our time on this
    beautiful earth is,
especially for those of us in our fifties and
    nearing sixty.
Wisdom, a knowingness, a helicopter view of
    the world are gifts you receive gratefully
    as you age.
You realize that spending time with the people
    you love and who love you back is
    everything.

We are both quiet,
We are both still,
for we know what we know.
And we take the time to let it sink in.

Missing you on weekends while you're at work is hard.
I spend the rest of the trip planning ways you could reach the end of your current project quicker so that you can spend more Saturdays with me.

THE FRIENDS WHO LIT MY WAY

Depression wouldn't let go.
It was holding on so tightly.
I would not know whence it came,
until I examined more carefully
the causes of my pain.

Welling up inside my chest
(the place where grief is stored)
was a cry so profound that
it shook me to the core.

And then I remembered:
I lost three friends this month.
Two before their time.
One who lingered longer.

These were not ordinary friends.
Oh no, quite the opposite.
They were extraordinary.
Their spirits shone brightly—

From each emanated the most beautiful light.
No wonder I am as sad as I am.

I clearly remember receiving the best from each
    of them . . .
A gentle kiss on a beaten-up porch from one.
Shared excitement and passion after seeing
    a Broadway play together from the second.
The third gave me the gift of joy when I needed
    it most; and the way he made me laugh
    will stay with me forever.

They loved me to the core, as I loved them,
And feeling their love was life affirming.

If I could speak to them just once more, I'd say,
'Thank you for loving me, and for lighting
    my way.'

BARE BRANCHES

I miss you in the mornings.
The bare, weathered branches on the trees
 outside our bedroom window seem to
 share my sadness as they await the rebirth
 of all things green, which is synonymous
 with Spring.
If they were lush with growth, perhaps I would
 gain some comfort.
But they are not.
As they wait for the new season to arrive, so
 must I be patient for you to return to me
 from work every evening.
I imagine, many years from now, these same
 low-bending branches looking for me
 inside our bedroom window and being
 saddened to learn I am no longer there.
Still, I take comfort in the idea that although I
 am gone then, these magnificent trees will
 still be living on this beautiful earth.

SOMETIMES

After I got over the guilt of not attending
    an event to which I'd RSVPed yes,
    it suddenly occurred to me—it hit me like
    a ton of bricks falling from the sky—
That I often do things I don't want to do
    just to please others.
Or because I don't want to let them down.
But sometimes we're not in the mood to do
    what others expect of us.
And that really is okay.
Sometimes, a person just wants to sit
    in a comfortable chair
And read a darn good book!

SLEEPING BEAUTY #2

Waking up from this restless slumber had not
    been in the forefront of my mind.
I was too preoccupied with fixing all that was
    wrong inside—and never ever saw the
    bigger picture.

I never knew all of what was in my inmost
    heart.
I buried it for too long, and felt like I was
    asleep for an eternity.

'Love is always the answer,' she whispered
    in my ear.
'Love is all that matters.'
At last I could finally hear her voice.

I'm awake for the very first time and
    it feels divine.
No more sinning mentality,
No keeping me down with archaic rules.
Jesus came to save humanity and break
    our karmic cycle.

It's time to rise up and claim our divinity,
Time to listen to the love that lives inside.

'Love is always the answer,' she whispered
    in my ear.
'Love is all that matters,' now I can finally hear.
'Love is always the answer,' she whispered
    in my ear.
'Love is all that matters,' and now I can finally
    hear.

YOUR EYES

For the first time, in a very long time
I cannot find the words.
They do not come, they do not flow
because your eyes have taken
my breath away—
perhaps just for a moment.
But nevertheless, I can't breathe.

When I do find my breath again
my breaths are slow, deep, steady.
Your eyes—
a deep, soulful blue—
transcend this lifetime, and the one before that,
and the one before that,
and awaken in me things I may have known
    about myself,
but buried deep, deep inside me,
for such a very long time.

The way time stops when you look at me,
and how my body trembles at the mere brush
    of your hand against mine,
I'd forgotten how that feels.
Your support reminds me of my courage.
How could I have forgotten that creativity is
    the essence of my soul?

BELONGING

'Bring back my ancestors,' I heard my family
　　cry. 'Bring them back to heal us.'
Then they sighed a sigh so strong it shook
　　the earth.
I have prayed out loud, hoping that somehow,
　　we can once again connect.
A whole generation of elders has passed away.
One by one they left us.
And my young brother, too, long before his time.
I have called out to them repeatedly,
'Nana, Dad, Domenic, please, come back to
　　heal us, so that somehow, we can once
　　again belong.'
But nothing has taken away my longing for
　　times past.
Belonging is a seed inside that yearns to grow,
　　it's a feeling within that Aunt Arlene, on the
　　other side, seems to understand, as she
　　guides us: mother, father, sister, brother,
　　children, cousins.

She guides the living, big and small,
and promises to lead us to a place we will one
 day know, where we feel peace deep within
 our souls.
But for now we must bear the burden of our
 human pain.
It's weird not to see people I've loved my whole,
 entire life.
But they are gone, and for a moment I forget,
And start to dial my father's number only to
 remember, *Oh yes, he is gone, he is no longer
 here, that vibrant man whose life force was
 huge, whose presence on Earth meant I
 always had a home to go back to, it's insane
 that he's gone.*
And I wonder, *Will I ever be able to fill
 that void?*

STILLNESS

I can hear them quake,
the bombs and the tanks.
I can hear them roar.
Even as the mystics and the sages
cry out to the world,
'What are you doing?'
flashes of light penetrate the night,
and send a message to us all:
'You will fall.
'You. Will. Fall.'

War never works.
We must stop these senseless conflicts.
Stand still a moment—
just one moment—
please.
Look at the trees
reaching high into the sky.
They are calm and tranquil,
without even trying.

Watching the trees, I am crying
because I know where we have gone wrong.
But I am one, not all, and who am I to stop wars?
I have heard a message from beyond the sky
where hopes and dreams are not a lie,
but rather, visions of a better life
not filled with so much pain and strife.
'Bring back the goddesses, the witches, and the sages.
Bring back the oracles and the wisdom of the ages.'
Stand still and breathe quietly.
Listen to the gentle rustle from the trees,
and let the peaceful breezes comfort you
while you sleep at night.
In the morning, the sun shines bright
and fills us with warmth so magnificent
that we believe we can put the world to right.
Please, please, stop senseless fighting,
I implore you.
The collective pain we feel is not something we can ignore.
Not for a moment longer.

CELESTIAL BLUE

I imagine for a moment that I am flying into
    the cerulean sky where Marc Chagall's
    paintings live.
I see them all—the lopsided houses,
the newlywed couple in a loving embrace,
a bouquet of magenta flowers whizzing by,
and the goat-faced human playing the cello.
And I consider, I contemplate, I carefully
    think about whether Chagall ever had
    dreams of flying.
How else could he have created such
    imaginative paintings, bursting with so
    much liveliness and vibrant color?
Perhaps he needed to paint these fanciful
    images to escape from the human
    monstrosity that we call *war*.

War means different things to different
    people;
it isn't always guns and bombs.

It could be the constant *ping, ping, ping* of
>hundreds of abusive texts you receive from an alcoholic family member whose sole intent is to destroy you.

That's what it is for me.

Not wanting to think about this attack,
>or to numb my pain with food, as I sometimes do,

I fly into Chagall's celestial blue sky and glide,
>alongside a bouquet of fragrant pink roses and a pair of lovers,
>
>and I imagine that I am the woman being embraced so lovingly by her soul mate for an eternity.

It's wonderful and exciting here.

AMAZING GRACE AND JULIET

You came to me in the middle of my line
'It is an honor that I dream not of.'
How was this possible? You had passed away
six months before.
I felt goosebumps on my arms and a voice
inside telling me to look to my right.
I turned my head and you were there, smack
dab in the middle of the audience, perfectly
dressed in your finest brown tweed blazer, a
wool skirt, and your favorite felt hat, which
half covered your ears and was rolled up
ever so slightly at the rim.
You were smiling from ear to ear. I remember
that smile, and how it had a way of lighting
up a room.
We had dedicated our production of *Romeo
and Juliet* to you, calling upon you to guide
us through every problem and challenge.

We called you our angel, so it shouldn't have been a surprise when you showed up so unexpectedly. (Without a ticket.)

I noticed the silk pink roses on your lapel.

Pink, your favorite color. The color of love, nurturing, and compassion.

The world stopped. Maybe just for a moment, but it felt like forever.

I gazed lovingly into your sparkling brown eyes and your smile melted my heart. And for a moment it was just you and me—no audience, no other actors—just us.

You stared into my eyes and emanated enough love to last me a lifetime. Then you winked at me, and in an instant, you were gone.

I gasped. I don't think anybody noticed. Not the audience. Not my Nurse or my Mother, the Lady Capulet.

My namesake, my Nana. my favorite person in the whole world, you were the one person in my life whose love I could always count on.

'I'll look to like, if looking liking move:
But no more deep will I endart mine eye
Than your consent gives strength to make it fly.'
   (Enter SERVINGMAN)

THE MIRACLE OF TREES

It was time to speak to the trees again.
I had so much to ask them,
and they had so much to say.

As I placed my palm on the flaking bark of an
 ancient yew tree,
I instantly felt a surge of healing energy
 emanating from my palm.
I was giving it to this tranquil tree, and it came
 back,
flowing into every part of me—an energy so
 strong it calmed me down.

I had recently read that the palms of our hands
are a powerful portal of connection to the
 heart chakra.
*Ah, now I understand. We are truly made of
 energy,* I thought.

I stood for a while in silence, with my arm
  outstretched
and my palm lovingly touching the peeling
  bark of this peaceful tree.
'You are a healer,' I said to the tree.
'Oh yes,' I imagined the tree replying. 'I am a
  wise old tree,
and I have much to give you, and you to me.'

As my breathing regulated, I breathed slow,
  steady breaths,
and was transported to a place deep within
  my core.
A transference of wisdom had taken place
  between this wise old tree and me.
I blessed my new friend, gave back to it all that
  it had given me,
and sent it love and wishes for health and
  longevity.
In that moment, I felt God, I felt love, and this
  comforted me.

I looked down at the path that lay ahead,
Covered with variegated leaves that had
 blended in with the rich, lush soil and
 ultrathin twigs.
I imagined it to be an autumnal collage
 of sorts.

How perfect nature is.
How do the leaves know to fall away in
 autumn and birth again in spring?
Can we do that, too?

Can all the hate, judgment, and nastiness in
 the world
fall away and transform itself into
a beautiful spring of rebirth and love?
I truly hope so.

HEALING

There comes a time when the January blues
 won't find you,
When the dull gray sky and the bitter cold
 won't get you down,
When the higher number on the scale won't
 make your heart sink to a place so low you
 fear you will never rise back up again.
There comes a time when everything won't
 seem so painful,
When your feelings of dread, despair, and
 depression will melt away as effortlessly as
 the sun melts the snow on a sunny day,
And instead of wishing for warmer weather
 and a clear blue sky, you accept what is.
On that day, you accept what is and embrace
 with curious wonder the steely gray sky that
 is winter in England.

On that day, you wake up for the very first time to a person you never met before,
The person that lived inside of you separate from all the trauma.
And that light, that beautiful soulful light that shone brightly in you as a baby, will shine once more,
But even brighter than ever before.
There will come a time when you stop fighting with everyone who verbally attacks you because you have healed yourself.
And you will no longer go into fight-or-flight mode.
You will realize there is an incredible power in not responding, and so you'll breathe and breathe.
You will take it all in, and smile to yourself.
Although you may never be good enough in others' eyes, there will come a day when you won't care anymore what they think because you have realized your value.
This is everything.
No more climbing up that mountain.

You will have weathered the storm, and come out on the other side more whole than you've ever been in your entire life.

NOTES

PREFACE

Epigraph. Plato. *The Apology of Socrates* (circa 399 BCE).

1. From an August 1, 2001, interview of Mary Oliver by Coleman Barks sponsored by the Lannan Foundation, available at Lannan.org.

ACKNOWLEDGMENTS

Matthew. My soul mate, the love of my life, thank you for your love, patience, and compassion. Thank you for believing in me when I didn't believe in myself, for listening to my poems, and most importantly, for loving them and me unconditionally. Thank you for always supporting my dreams, fully without hesitation. Brushing my hand with yours still gives me goosebumps. Can I just hold your hand forever, please?

Emma. My beautiful daughter, I waited a long time for you and I'm so happy you chose me to be your mom. I was in love with you from the moment I saw your fiery red hair and looked into your sparkling blue eyes. I was thrilled to have given birth to a ginger. I knew you were going to do great things from the moment you were born. I learn invaluable lessons from you, and for this I am grateful. You always inspire me. Being a mother to you has filled my heart and touched my soul in ways I never knew were possible. Keep shining your magnificent light and never stop believing in your dreams. By shining your light, you inspire everyone around you to shine theirs and the world needs more of this.

Stephanie Gunning. Thank you for editing my poems and convincing me the best way forward was to independently publish. You are an extraordinary editor and I'm so happy I found you again after so many years. It was meant to be and I'm grateful to you for believing in my writing. Working with you makes me feel seen, heard, and respected. This is everything. Your dedication, commitment, wisdom, and patience are qualities that you embody which make you the brilliant editor and production manager that you are. Thank you from my whole heart and soul for helping to make my dream a reality.

Annie, Debbie, Brenda, Paula, Patty, Alicia, and Elizabeth—friends who light my way. As my friends for life, you have a big place in my heart. Thank you for believing in my creative gifts and for your love and support.

Eleanor. Thank you for your support, love, and thoughtfulness, which mean so much to me.

Sylvie. Thank you for your kindness and for calling me "Darling Grace." You can't imagine how those words have lifted me. Such a simple thing has touched my heart on so many occasions.

Laura. Thank you for the poetry books, which translates to thoughtfulness in my book.

Marybeth. My childhood "bestie," thank you for coming into my life at such an early age and for your steadfast friendship. You threw me a buoy just in time.

Helen, Lizzie, Mandy, Janine, and Julia. Thank you for listening to me read my poems aloud and for your friendship, which I treasure.

Tess and Sally. I appreciate your love, support, and beautiful friendship. Your positive response to my poems in the beginning gave me the encouragement I needed to continue writing.

Jossi. Thank you for always staying on the sunny side of life. And for your positive outlook. Thank you also to Boomer and Minnie for always being so happy to see me—dogs can lift us in ways I never knew possible. They heal us.

Marion. Thank you for loving my poem "To My Love," which is now "Instructions," and for reading it at your precious sister's funeral. You read it so beautifully that I now, on occasion, imagine your sister swirling in the sky with the birds filled with joy and this makes me smile.

Nana. My angel in heaven, thank you for teaching me what pure love is by your example and for loving me when I needed it the most. I miss you beyond words.

Dad. You're in heaven. "What's the Rush" and "The Grief That Lives Inside" express how much I love you. You, like Nana, are missed beyond words.

Domenic. Dying so young taught me how short and precious life is and not to take anything for granted. Your death also made me examine my fear of dying, and by doing so, freed me from debilitating fear and opened up a whole new perspective of life for me. Thank you, my sweet brother. Thank you for sharing your poems with me when we were kids, and for that time you spoke to me.

Nicholas. Thank you for reading my poems, for your constant love and support, and for being an amazing cousin through the years. You have such a beautiful soul, and I love you.

Carmel. Thank you for reminding us of the gift of gratitude that you embody so beautifully on a daily basis. I love you.

Valerie. You have a beautiful heart and remind me of our nana. Thank you for being an extension of her and for all of the lightness you bring to the world and to me.

Mom. Thank you for always saying Domenic's death was a gift. You started a journey after he passed and I paid attention. You recently said to me "suffering is good for the soul; this is where growth takes place. People come into our lives so that we can grow and develop." We learn so much from each other. Thank you for seeking, as it had a ripple effect on everyone around you. My heart is full.

Sally. My fun-loving sister, thank you for your support and unconditional love, and always making me laugh. You are one of a kind, Sally Girl.

Dina. You are such a beautiful mother and I have learned so much from you, and for this I am grateful.

Jackie. My lovely sister-in-law, from the very beginning you were supportive and listened with love to me reading my poems aloud. Thank you for your encouragement and for cheering me on. You have a very special place in my heart.

Martha. My guide, my angel, your wise and beautiful soul has taught me how to navigate the difficult moments of my life along with the joyful moments. I am grateful to you for all the lives we have known each other.

Emily Grace. Thank you for editing my first poem. You are brilliant and wise and a beautiful light in the world.

Gail. Thank you for your love and support and for our long, healing talks on the phone, which I will always treasure.

Lisa E. Thank you for our impromptu Facebook chats which always, without fail, lift my spirits. We have been connected since the day we were born.

Jane. My acting partner-in-crime, playing giggling girls at the Actors Studio another lifetime ago. Thank you for listening to and reading my poems, supporting my dreams, and your encouragement and love.

Jennifer. Thank you for always being so positive and for encouraging me. You and Jane are my "sisters from another mister." Love you.

Ignazio. Your positive approach to everything you do is contagious. Thank you for making me laugh during the difficult times and for making real estate so much fun even when it's hard.

Doug. Thank you for your wise and loving guidance, for being a channel for angelic healing and for assisting me in healing myself. You have a big place in my heart.

Cousins. So many of you have brought healing and light to my life and I'm grateful to each and every one of you. You know who you are.

Phoebe Thank you, my tech savvy friend for creating my website and teaching me how to post on Instagram. You're an absolute pleasure to work with and your calm demeanor and can-do attitude is greatly appreciated.

To the lovely staff at **The Natural Food Deli,** thank you for always greeting me with a big smile and for creating such a wholesome environment.

ABOUT THE AUTHOR

GRACE MIGLIO PEARCE is an actor, film producer, and poet. She divides her time between Hampshire, England, where she lives with her husband, Matthew Pearce, and Long Island, New York, in the United States. They share a grown daughter, Emma.

Printed in Dunstable, United Kingdom